Adrienne Jerratt

Pastoral Care

of

Children

D1798456

and

Young People

Quaker Books

First published in July 2001 by
Quaker Books, Friends House, Euston Road,
London NW1 2BJ

Pastoral care
of
children and young people

First published in July 2001 by Quaker Books, Friends
House, Euston Road, London NW1 2BJ

ISBN 0 85245 331 0

Printed by Thanet Press Ltd.

CONTENTS

Pastoral care of children and young people

Introduction

Rejoice in the presence of children and young people in your meeting and recognise the gifts they bring. Remember that the meeting as a whole shares a responsibility for every child in its care. Seek for them as for yourself a full development of God's gifts and the abundant life Jesus tells us can be ours. How do you share your deepest beliefs with them, while leaving them free to develop as the spirit of God may lead them? Do you invite them to share their insights with you? Are you ready both to learn from them and to accept your responsibilities towards them?

Quaker faith & practice 1.19[1]

Children and young people are important members of our meeting communities. They are individuals, each with their own needs and gifts. How can we reflect this in our provision of pastoral care?

In 1997 seven young Friends, three members of Quaker Home Service[2] Children & Young People's Committee, and two staff from Children & Young People's Section met to discuss issues of relevance to young people in the Religious Society of Friends in Britain. This group, the Quaker Youth Forum (QYF), identified oversight of children and young people as

---

[1] *Details of this and other publications can be found in Appendix 3: Resources, page 40.*

[2] *This department of the Religious Society of Friends in Britain (Quakers) is now called Quaker Life. Addresses and other contact details for all groups and organisations mentioned can be found on page 45.*

important to young Friends. It expressed concern about current systems of oversight, and asked Children & Young People's Committee to take the matter forward.

Later in 1997 several members of QYF presented a session on oversight of children and young people at Quaker Home Service Representative Council. In 1999 the Committee on Eldership & Oversight and Children & Young People's Committee held a joint conference on oversight of children and young people. As a result of that conference, the two committees have produced this booklet in the handbook series for those responsible for eldership and oversight in local meetings.

In an all-age worshipping community it is hard to separate eldership from oversight. They are inextricably linked. As children and young people develop as individuals their spiritual and pastoral needs cannot be separated.

Pastoral care of children and young people has its own particular difficulties and rewards, and the purpose of this booklet is to help Friends in thinking about how to offer oversight and eldership with children and young people. It does not claim to have all the answers, but it may help to clarify the issues and provide a starting point for discussions in meetings.

This booklet aims to provide useful background reading for elders and overseers, monthly meeting children and young people's resource co-ordinators, members of children and young people's committees in monthly or preparative meetings, Friends who help with children's meetings and other events, and any other interested Friends. We are all to take a 'right share in the privilege of watching over one another for good', as *Quaker faith & practice* chapter 12.19 (*Qfp*) reminds us. In this book we use 'elders' or 'overseers' as shorthand for all who undertake the responsibility seriously and with commitment, whether their meeting makes formal appointments or shares the tasks corporately.

It is suggested that one or more adult friends and at least one young person read this document on behalf of the preparative meeting, and report back with suggestions as to how it may be used in the context of their particular meeting. It is hoped that the booklet will facilitate discussion on how to explore the issue of pastoral care of children and young people and how to bring about appropriate changes to improve it, integrating it within the life of the meeting.

All aspects of guidance given in *Quaker faith & practice* on responsibilities of eldership (12.12) and oversight (12.13) have relevance for children and young people. All in the community are encouraged to play their part in eldership and oversight. Consideration should be given to how children and young people can and do contribute to these functions. They may already play a significant role in pastoral care, particularly of each other, as well as in the spiritual life of the community as a whole.

Helping Friends of all ages to communicate with each other is important in building the community. Communication is based on **listening** to each other. Sometimes we need to adapt our language so that we can be understood. The process is made easier as Friends share opportunities to **do** things together.

- How would each part of *Qfp* 12.12(a-l) and 12.13(a-q) apply to children and young people? How could they play an active role, caring as well as being cared for?

- What opportunities are there in your meeting for all-age sharing of activities and responsibilities?

Creating a framework

To underpin the most important aspects of pastoral care (such as welcoming children and young people into the meeting and developing a sense of community) each meeting needs a framework of safety. When such a framework for pastoral care is in place, Friends are enabled to build relationships and enjoy their journeys together. The framework will provide a sense of security and support for all involved, knowing what is expected of them and where they can go for help and support. It is important that no-one is out on a limb without the support of other Friends or feels overburdened. The sharing of experience and discussion of mutual problems should be built into the pastoral care system with courses and conferences at local, regional and national levels.

> *Every morning during the winter months I restructure our wood fire, which has been sleeping overnight. Some dead ash is removed; the glowing embers are pulled forward to prominence and the burnable wood placed in contact with them. Structure allows for easy spreading from the spark or ember throughout the whole fire. The pieces nearest the embers need to be easily combustible to transfer greater heat to more solid logs.*
>
> Tony Habgood, at the conference on
> oversight of children and young people

In our meetings we want to create a structure which allows the easy flow of ideas, enthusiasms, requests, questions, and cries for help or of anger between children and young people and the whole body of the membership of the meeting.

Any framework will include appointments made (see Appendix 2), patterns of communication, and guidelines established. The exact form of the framework used in each of our various monthly and preparative meetings will vary. It will certainly need to be flexible and responsive to the changing needs of the children and young people associated with our meetings and the fluctuating availability of resources.

Communication between all those working with children and young people is essential. It allows people to share problems and useful ideas and it can be both a safety net and a source of fresh inspiration. However, it may not always be clear what information should be communicated and what should be kept confidential. Meetings may have agreed their own policies on confidentiality, but some general points about communication could be borne in mind.

Communication of general problems may often be useful. Wherever appropriate, describe a situation without identifying the people concerned. The needs of the hearer to share and be supported should also be considered.

Confidential information should be passed on to parents only in exceptional circumstances. After all, parents would not expect Friends to tell their children about their problems; there must be an equal respect for their children's desire for confidentiality.

If a child or young person discloses emotional, physical, or sexual abuse, this information must not be kept confidential. An adult must pass on information which could stop someone being harmed and should not, therefore, promise confidentiality. However, the information should only be shared with those who need to know for the good of the child concerned. It is important to think through in advance how a Friend would handle the disclosure of abuse; the booklet *Meeting safety* (see below) provides useful guidance for meetings thinking about these difficult issues.

Meeting safety

Guidelines can help ensure the safety of children, young people, and adults. The booklet *Meeting safety* is an essential resource for meetings. It is an amalgamation of the earlier publications *Health, safety and the law* and *Safeguarding children from harm*, and conforms to changes in the law up to the year 2001. It aims to provide guidance to those who work with children and young people, offering examples of good practice and suggesting how to provide a safe environment for all concerned.

- Has everyone involved in work with children and young people in the meeting read and considered the book *Meeting safety*, noting the changes from previous booklets?
- Have children and young people been involved in the discussion of safety issues?
- Does the meeting have its own guidelines on the care of children and young people? Are these guidelines formally agreed, clear and well publicised?
- What sorts of activity might help stimulate useful discussion within the whole meeting? Perhaps children and young people might make a poster to illustrate meeting house 'rules' and other measures for their safety, following a discussion on the topic. This would include advice on how to contact an appropriate adult to talk about any concerns.
- Who has overall responsibility to make sure agreed principles are kept in mind, and agreed practice is adhered to?
- Are helpers given support?

If the meeting has had clear and well publicised guidelines for some time, it may still be helpful periodically to offer discussion groups or training sessions on child protection and general safety issues. It is important to work through the policy carefully with any adults new to work with children and young people. Children & Young People's Section can provide training.

Meeting safety stresses the need for children and young people to have an independent person they can talk to, see Appendix 2 on children's overseers.

Welcoming children and young people

All newcomers, including children and young people, should be welcomed into the meeting. First impressions are important, and someone who feels unwelcome on their first visit may not return. With smaller children it is important that their parents feel comfortable with any arrangements for their care, for example while their parents are in the adult meeting for worship.

- How can you communicate a welcome which says, 'You are valued and we wish to help you develop your gifts'? What messages are given by your noticeboard and entrance area? Try viewing the meeting house from the point of view of a child. No-one should go from a meeting feeling that they are not important. Are children and young people encouraged to sign the visitors' book, and do they receive a follow-up postcard too? The children's room should be a special place suited to their needs and not simply a back room chosen so that the children won't disturb the meeting.

- What provision is there for children and young people who turn up unexpectedly? Would the person on welcoming duty at the door know what action would be required of them, or whom they could ask for support?

- How can children and young people who do not attend regularly be encouraged to feel welcome? Might it be appropriate to send invitations for special events?

Young people greatly appreciate efforts made to remember their personal details and circumstances. Being remembered gives a feeling of belonging.

Adults should be aware that comments such as 'How nice to see young people in our meeting', though kindly meant, can sound patronising. We all want to be welcomed as ourselves, not as representatives of a social group.

Remember that the more cohesive a group feels to those who are a part of it, the more impenetrable or like a 'clique' it may look to those who are looking at it from the outside. If this is a situation that might arise in your meeting, consider how it might be avoided. It may be a good idea to discuss (or act out) welcoming newcomers or occasional visitors in the children's regular meetings. Asking the children and young people what they think they could do to welcome others to the meeting will help them to understand that it is their responsibility too.

- How easy is it for new attenders to feel at home and get to know who to ask for advice, support or guidance? If a meeting has designated overseers and elders with special responsibility for children and young people, it is important that they are introduced. It might be appropriate to display their photographs. Some meetings display photographs of all elders and overseers, or even of all members (making sure, however, that the addresses of vulnerable people are not publicised).

- Is there a system for following up letters of introduction, e.g. for young people who may have moved into your area to follow a course of education, or to work? What information might be useful to them, and how might they be helped to access it?

- Is there a time other than Sunday mornings for young people to join with you for worship or other activities? For many young people Sunday morning is a time for sleep, homework, or a paid job. If your meeting house is inaccessible without a car, an alternative venue might also be considered.

- How should any unwelcoming behaviour by 'regular' children towards a newcomer or irregular visitor be dealt with? It may or may not be intentional, and can happen as a result of high spirits or thoughtlessness, but the newcomer's sensitivities should be acknowledged and more considerate behaviour asked for.

Developing a sense of community

Our life is love, and peace, and tenderness; and bearing one with another, and forgiving one another, and not laying accusations one against another; but praying for one another, and helping one another up with a tender hand.

Isaac Penington, 1667, Qfp 10.01

A sense of community gives the Society its life. In order to care for each other and have opportunities to give and receive our own spiritual and pastoral nurturing we need to know each other. This is easier when we do things together, adults as well as the young.

- How often do Friends do things together, besides meeting for worship? Do these activities include social, leisure, and work activities?
- Do Friends remember to celebrate good news and joy with each other as well as sorrows and difficulties?
- At specially organised social events such as birthday parties, picnics, or talks, it might be helpful for Friends to wear name badges. These could include the answer to a simple question (for example, 'which person in Quaker history/the Bible/the Harry Potter books/... would you most like to have a one-to-one with?') to break the ice and stimulate discussion.
- Do, or should, all adults consider it part of their responsibility to include children and young people in the life of the meeting?

Consider how children and young people might be integrated into the life of the meeting. There may well be practical tasks in the meeting which they can get involved in. Consider asking children and young people if they would like to help with welcoming adult Friends, with the flowers, or with the coffee after meeting. It is important to show children and young people that the adults do see them as part of the community of the meeting. They should not be isolated from the meeting in an attempt to keep them 'safe', or only allowed to interact with a few 'approved' adults. Different situations may require different provision for children and young people. Being known, integrated, loved and respected is also a means of safety, and vital to their growth towards maturity. Meetings have to consider how to apply the *Meeting safety* guidelines flexibly in their own circumstances so they are comfortable as well as safe, like car seat-belts rather than shackles.

- It is easier for people of all ages to feel a part of the community when they join activities regularly. What can be done to help irregular attenders to feel they are part of a caring community?
- Does the meeting rely over-heavily on one person or a small group of people to organise and run children and young people's activities? Are other Friends encouraged to take their turn, even if for just a part of a session, or to share a session with a regular helper?
- What steps are taken to help adults know what goes on in children's meetings? How much status is given to the children and young people's activities? Consider ways in which the children and young people's activities can be integrated into the life of the wider meeting, and how members not directly involved can be kept informed. Is there an opportunity for children and young people to report on what they have been doing? Consider displaying their work in a central area of the meeting house, producing a children's meeting newsletter or web page, or offering children the chance to speak during the notices.
- What opportunities are there for all Friends to get to know each other in the 'things that are eternal'? Is

there a willingness to use these times to listen to each other?

If your meeting sends children and young people birthday cards, consider how this is done, and how the cards are received. Are they warmly welcomed or seen merely as empty gestures? To what age should the practice continue?

Worshipping together

> *Our testimonies arise from our way of worship. Our way of worship evokes from deep within us at once an affirmation and a celebration, an affirmation of the reality of that Light which illuminates the spiritual longing of humanity, and a celebration of the continual resurrection within us of the springs of hope and love; a sense that each of us is, if we will, a channel for a power that is both within us and beyond us.*
>
> *Lorna M Marsden, 1986* Qfp 20.16

The Quaker community is based on shared worship. To maintain this for people at all ages and stages of religious development, we may need to provide varied opportunities for worship open to all. These may include silent worship, silent worship with a programmed reading, worship sharing (encouraging ministry), worship through a range of activities, and ministry on specific topics and expressed in different ways. An invitation to express prayer in written words, drawing, modelling or spoken words can be included in a period of worship. The resources list at the end of this booklet (page 34) gives some further suggestions including exploring all-age worship. Your monthly meeting resource coordinator will have a wealth of information and ideas to offer. Are there particular opportunities locally? In some meeting houses there may be different groups worshipping in different ways at the same time, using varied modes of expression and styles of language.

- Do you recognise children's meetings as meetings for worship? (What message is given if we call it a children's 'class'?)
- How important is our form of worship in defining us as a religious community? Are we open to trying 'non-traditional' forms of worship? Remember that Friends in other yearly meetings may worship in different ways from Quakers in Britain.
- Do we make assumptions about the form of worship in which children, young people or adults may wish to take part at any specific time?

Channels of communication

> If we take seriously the nurture of our children in the worshipping group, we must start by re-appraising the whole life of the group. What kind of communication exists between us all? Do we know one another as people sharing joys and sorrows?
>
> Peggy McGeoghegan, 1976 Qfp 10.10

Channels of communication between young people and adults in the meeting are essential to help young people to feel valued. It takes time for a level of trust to develop, and in order for this to happen young people need to feel that their concerns are of interest to adults and will be taken seriously. Opportunities for communication therefore need to be created, and to be taken when they arise.

Sharing activities and other non-verbal communication can be of great value to children and adults. Shared humour, creativity and fun can be effective means to opening and maintaining channels of communication.

- How might it be possible to encourage an awareness that other ways of communicating than just words can be effective?
- Are children and young people aware of the needs and feelings of older people in the meeting? How can their understanding of and sense of responsibility towards all Friends be fostered? Could children and young people be included in visits to Friends who are ill?

Some Friends may need reassurance or even guidance if they feel they 'aren't good with children and young people'. Not everyone is going to be able or willing to assist with children's activities, but all can share mutual respect and friendliness.

Linked Friends

Most meetings are familiar with the various appointments that could be made: children and young people's committees, convenors of these committees, at preparative or monthly meeting level, resource coordinators, helpers with the children's meeting, and children's overseers. All these roles have proved their worth, and meetings are encouraged to include them on the regular list of appointments to be made. Appendix 2, page 34, describes their functions and responsibilities. Meetings may adapt the role descriptions to suit the circumstances of their meeting and the people available to carry out the tasks, reviewing the meeting's practice at regular intervals. However they re-combine or re-name other tasks, that of being an independent person (usually a children's overseer) must be kept clear.

'Linked Friends' are comparatively new under that name, though many people have been grateful for godparents, mentors, great-aunts and other older adults who have taken a special interest in them. This section describes the role in some detail, therefore.

Time and consistency are needed if an adult in meeting from outside the family is to develop a relationship with a child or young person and build up a degree of trust. The conventional overseer role may not allow for this, if overseers change triennially. If overseers have a dozen or more people, or whole families, on their 'list' they may not get a chance to know the children and young people individually, apart from occasional brief conversations after meeting for worship. This, of course, is a perennial challenge for all Friends and those they oversee. Corporate systems can overcome this problem to some extent, but care is still needed to see children as individuals and to link them sensitively. The appointment of a children's overseer (see Appendix 2, page 35) is very helpful, but children and young people at the 1997 Quaker Home Service Representative Council and at the conferences said they would value a friendship that is special and lasting, beyond triennial service.

Some meetings have developed a system of 'Linked Friends'. Children and young people are invited to be involved in choosing an adult member to be their own Linked Friend – someone who takes a special interest in them and with whom they feel comfortable. This means that a child or young person has someone with whom they can build up a relationship over a long period of time, and the continuity makes it far easier to maintain channels of communication, even through periods of infrequent attendance at meeting for worship. This relationship will only work when both people in the link feel comfortable and safe: it will be necessary to ensure that the system is well structured and effectively monitored. The scheme will need one or more co-ordinators to arrange the pairings and then to monitor the progress of the scheme. The co-ordinators could ask participating children and young people to name two or more people they would like to be linked with and then approach the named people to see if they feel able to take on the responsibility. It is important that no one feels overburdened. For very small children the parents may wish to suggest a Linked Friend on their behalf. Parental support for participation in the Linked Friends system is essential.

The purpose of a Linked Friends scheme is to introduce a child or young person to one adult, and to use that relationship to build links with the whole meeting. The closeness between the two halves of the link should not be exclusive, and the co-ordinator of the scheme should establish careful ground rules for all concerned, including advice about confidentiality. Where the pairs decide to meet informally it would be a good idea to include others involved in the scheme. Where a group of adults meet with a group of children and young people, there is more chance for sharing and getting to know each other, and there is a back-up system in case of injury or accident. Linked Friends should be sure to study 'A code of good practice for volunteers working on children and young people's events in Britain Yearly Meeting' in *Meeting safety*.

Linked Friends might get to know each other in a variety of ways. For example:

- After meeting, talk about what happened in children's meeting and in the main meeting. The adult might consider attending children's meeting.
- At residential or mixed age events make time to meet and talk.
- Exchange e-mail messages and postcards or letters, especially if either one cannot come to meeting regularly.
- Share favourite books.
- If the adult has a special responsibility in the meeting

such as welcoming newcomers, the child or young person could help.

- The child or young person could be included in the welcome visit to new members.
- The child or young person could accompany the adult serving on a stall/serving coffee/supporting the meeting in another practical way. Similarly the pair could collaborate on charity or community work.
- Share hobbies and interests.
- Celebrate each other's birthdays.
- Organise an outing or event in conjunction with other pairs of Linked Friends.

Meetings could consider the desirability and/or feasibility of setting up a Linked Friends system in their meeting. Would it be helpful to talk to someone who has experience of the system? For example, Edinburgh Central and Rugby Preparative Meetings operate this system, can speak of the benefits and discuss any worries about safety.

- Do the children and young people in your meeting get to know enough adults to be able to choose a Linked Friend, if they wished? If not, how can this situation be changed?

Enabling spiritual development, growth and change

> *I should like to change the name 'seekers' to 'explorers'. There is a considerable difference there: we do not seek the Atlantic, we explore it. The whole field of religious experience has to be explored, and has to be described in a language understandable to modern men and women.*
>
> Ole Olden, 1955 Qfp 26.17

A Quaker meeting should be a place where the spiritual needs of children and young people are nurtured.

Although young people might not raise spiritual issues themselves without encouragement, that should not be taken to mean they are not interested. Almost all children get a general religious education in school and will have their own ideas and feelings about this, as well as their own private queries. In such a secular society as ours it is difficult for children and young people to broach topics seen as spiritual or religious, and they should be encouraged to feel that Friends are people with whom they can explore these issues. If they can't do it at meeting and Quaker events, where can they? Learning to express one's own beliefs and listen to the points of view of others, beyond their own families, is an integral part of our spiritual growth and development.

- Are you clear on your meeting's aims for the children and young people's meeting? (*Firm foundations* (see Appendix 3 page 41) has exercises to help draw these out.

- Do children and young people's meetings include topics such as aspects of spirituality, and Quaker history and beliefs, according to their age and level of development? Or is the focus mainly on environmental, cross-cultural topics, social and craft activities? Drama, role play, and creative activities can be effective in making aspects of Quaker history and testimonies come alive. Children & Young People's Section can help with activity suggestions, including ways to explore *Quaker faith & practice*.

- Could adult members of meeting be encouraged to talk to the children and young people about their own spiritual journeys, or how they apply their spiritual beliefs in their work and daily lives? This could be done in all-age worship, or in the children and young people's meetings. Honest sharing of questions and doubts can be immensely helpful to young people.

- Are periods of silence integrated into the children and young people's meetings? Are you flexible in accepting children and young people in a meeting for worship based on silence for the time they feel comfortable? The age of the young people may affect how long they wish to stay in meeting (teenagers may want to stay longer than toddlers).

- How does your meeting room look and feel from a child's view point? As well as *Quaker faith & practice* and the Bible, do you have available some materials accessible to children? What could be done to make the experience of being in meeting for worship more comfortable and enjoyable for a child?

- What opportunities can be taken to give children and young people an introduction to Quaker business methods? (See also 'Business Meetings', page 28.)

Some meetings present *Quaker faith & practice* or another book – or a video or other appropriate gift – on a young person's 16th birthday, or perhaps the 12th or 18th birthday. Such a gift may be appreciated even by those young people who do not attend meeting very often. Contact Children & Young People's Section for suggested titles.

Responding to the needs of the individual

We are all, adults, children, and young people, individuals with unique experiences and unique perspectives. We all wish to be valued for who we are, and not to be pigeon-holed or categorised according to our age, sex, race, social class, disability, level of academic attainment, family, accent, or where we live. Although it is a natural human trait to group together those with obviously similar characteristics to some extent, it is something to be wary of as disrespectful and potentially very hurtful. Adults have a special responsibility to be sensitive to the needs and experiences of children and young people, and to avoid making assumptions based on incomplete information. Avoid gestures which may be seen as mere tokens, such as repeatedly asking a person to be a representative of a racial or social group, rather than to be himself or herself.

Adults responsible for organising activities should take care to liaise fully with children, young people, and parents to make sure that the needs of all are being met. This is especially important where children and young people with special needs are concerned. Many seemingly insoluble problems can be overcome through creative thinking and the use of shared or group problem-solving techniques. It is perhaps of greatest importance that the parents or young people themselves feel that Friends have approached any problems with open minds and loving hearts. When responding to young people's needs, don't be embarrassed to ask for clarification of their requirements or preferences, rather than making assumptions which may turn out to be wrong. It is better to ask if they are willing and able to do a task or join an activity than to make the decision for them by not asking at all.

Bullying, or the possibility of it, is something all adults involved in children and young people's activities should be sensitive to. It may or may not be conscious and deliberate, but in any case it needs to be tackled. There are several good publications that explore different methods of handling such situations. The Resources Room at Friends House or local libraries will have suggestions.

- How would adult helpers or parents go about handling situations where they feel bullying is or may be taking place? What action would children and young people feel able to take if they had similar concerns or felt themselves to be victims?

The children's meeting

> *I recall a family weekend, when the children, about twenty-four of them, aged three and upwards, had their own sessions in parallel to the adults. On the first evening, after the getting-to-know-you games, we sat down on the carpet to worship. We lit some candles on the hearth, turned off the lights, asked two children to be elders, and were still. The meeting went on for over a quarter of an hour, and was very deep. Then the two elders shook hands, but the silence continued. After another five minutes, I started a conversation, but no-one responded to my cheerful comments. I was the one who had lost touch. When the children did speak, it was slowly, thoughtfully, with long spaces between. This was when I realised that children do minister… That meeting lasted until someone entered the room and interrupted us – about forty-five minutes.*
>
> *Anne Hosking, 1984* Qfp 2.76

The children's meeting can be a prime forum for establishing channels of communication. It is an opportunity for worship, nurture, fun, friendship, learning and joy. It should not be left to parents to organise, but it should be the responsibility of the whole meeting to find those who can gather resources and help to plan and arrange the children and young people's meetings.

Those who work with children need to be able to communicate using any of the languages open to the child: play, drama, graphics, and music as well as words, and at the appropriate level. Do not forget body language – getting to the child's level is a physical as well as an intellectual task so we may all end up sitting on the floor!

- Is there someone or a small group of people who have responsibility for organising children and young people's meetings?
- Is this group or person well supported with materials, space, other people they can call on for help, and other resources they require?
- How are they supported and linked to the whole meeting?
- Would it be useful for the children's meetings to link up with children's meetings in your monthly meeting area? What would be the advantages of this and, if desirable, how could it be arranged?
- Consider what topics to cover in a year or other suitable period. How can plans be flexible enough to include and adapt to ideas coming from the young people themselves? Do they allow for ideas to develop over a period of weeks?
- How can the meeting's resources be best utilised? What might other members and attenders have to offer, perhaps in the way of sharing their experiences or skills?

Link Groups

Link Groups for teenagers are appreciated and remembered by many. Link Groups offer an important step on the way to the wider Quaker world.

As children, they probably met in their 'home' meeting, usually on Sundays for an hour or so. They may have joined monthly meeting camps or gone to Yearly Meeting with their parents. Now, they want to look further, widening horizons, taking more responsibility for their own activities and their spiritual journeys, but still within a safe, Friendly framework. Beyond Link Groups, there will be regional or national events that they can choose to join and, once they are eighteen, Young Friends General Meeting.

Opportunities to meet together with others of a similar age help to keep communication flowing at a time when self-confidence can be under attack, and when young people are exploring their own ideas, feelings and identities. In areas where numbers are limited it may be necessary to link up young people of the same age across a wider area, such as the monthly or general meeting area. Over the years the numbers of teenagers in a meeting may change, and Link Groups may need to be re-formed. In some areas Link Groups for 12 to 18 year olds undertake a wide range of activities. Meeting with other young Friends who have similar values and beliefs often provides a place where the young people can be themselves and talk in a way they wouldn't in other peer circles.

- Young people of this age are exploring their own ideas, feelings and identities. What opportunities can you provide to help this process be a positive and creative experience for the young people in your meeting?
- The age group 12 to 18 years is very wide and their interests are very varied – is it possible to find the resources to provide different activities for different age groups?

- How can opportunities be offered for young people to gain a wider view of the Quaker network as they mature? See, for example, the young people's calendar in *Quaker news*, nomination to conferences, summer schools and Junior Yearly Meeting.

- Consider the nominations procedure for young people's events. Informal systems can sometimes lead to unfairness, with the children of less well-known Friends being disadvantaged. Is the monthly meeting children and young people's resource co-ordinator involved? It may be appropriate to ask young people to suggest names since they may know of young Friends who are active in the local Link Group, though they do not often attend meeting on a Sunday.

Oversight of children and young people at residential events

Residential events for young Quakers can be important for their spiritual growth and integration into the Quaker community. On many occasions, young Friends will come to Quaker residential events wanting to release the pressure of everyday life and express their feelings. The creation of a strong community at an event can lead young people to want to share some of their most personal hopes and difficulties. It is important to think carefully about the arrangements for oversight at a residential event, perhaps discussing plans with the children's overseer. It may be appropriate for the organising team to take on the task of oversight at a particular event or it may be useful to have separate overseers and organisers. Young people may themselves be overseers; for example, Warwickshire Junior Young Friends have two 'listening points' (young people who act as overseers).

Being an overseer at residential events is a big responsibility, as well as being very rewarding, and needs to be thought about carefully. Those thinking of taking on the

role of overseer at a residential event could ask themselves the following questions:

- What do you feel you can give as an overseer?
- What are your aims for the role?
- What are your strengths and weaknesses?
- What will you find easy?
- What will you find difficult?
- Where do you find rewards and benefits in the role?
- Do you know your limits? Do you know what to do if the limits are passed?
- When a young person has a problem, do you give it as much weight as they do? No problem is 'too small'.
- Are you aware of the diversity of young peoples' concerns? How do you value this diversity?
- Have you thought about your language? Is it accept-able to the people you will be talking to?
- Have you gained as much information about potential problems and special needs from the participants as possible? The parents or carers of each young person should have signed a consent and medical form before the event. These forms should help alert the organising team to possible difficulties.
- Have you discussed with your fellow overseers what responsibility you may have for participants' misbehaviour? What are the possible causes of misbe-haviour? How will you manage it?

The role is not only serious conversations, but informal and fun too.

It would be useful to know who young people could be referred on to for counselling or other support. A simple guide to responding, a kind of 'first aid', called *One way of helping* (see Resources page 40) is available from Children & Young People's Section.

Remember that an overseer is:

- **not** a counsellor or a social worker.
- **not** expected to know all the answers.

Planning and preparation

Overseers should not be rushed off their feet with planning and organisation! Good preparation and support structures are essential.

- How many overseers will be required for the event? Ideally there should be at least one male and one female.
- Has the organising team discussed boundaries, including confidentiality, in the planning stage? Will they be acceptable to participants? Remember to take the law and your responsibility into account. (See *Meeting safety* for details on the limits of confidentiality).

It is important to discuss boundaries with the participants at the beginning of the event. Participants should understand that boundaries exist to make sure that the event is safe and comfortable for everyone. Open discussion will hopefully help young people to understand the reasons for the boundaries of the event and therefore encourage them to keep them.

- Are the overseers and organisers familiar with the meeting's *Meeting safety* policy? Familiarity is important to protect the adults as much as the child or young person.
- How are overseers supported? Do they know where to turn if they feel unable to deal with a situation?

  Adult helpers should remember that they are there to

support the children and young people, and integrate socially with them, not form a separate group.

After the event

It is often beneficial for participants and organisers to complete an evaluation at the end of the event, either individually or in a group. Useful questions include:

- What were the strengths and weaknesses of the event?
- What was good about the event and should be repeated?
- Was there a situation that could have been handled differently?
- What might you do differently next time?
- What have you learned?

Continuity of oversight between residential events and meeting

Residential events are times when young people may want to talk about issues in their personal lives. They may return full of enthusiasm, ready to apply for membership, with a burden of anxiety, or a mixture of feelings. Overseers at the event should be sensitive to the young person's need for confidentiality, but they may sometimes feel that it is appropriate to suggest sharing the problem with someone in the local meeting. Except where the young person is at risk (as explained in the booklet *Meeting safety*), any follow-up should be done only with their permission. Overseers might offer to contact someone in the meeting on the young person's behalf, but they should not do so without the young person's explicit consent. Links should be developed between local meetings and those involved in oversight at residential events, but sharing of particular issues will not always be appropriate.

- How do we provide continuity of concern without intrusion?

- How do we affirm, with sensitivity, what was good about an event?
- Will someone make a point of discussing residential events with young people before they leave and/or on their return? If not a Linked Friend, then who?

In addition to issues of pastoral care, organisers of residential events should ensure that local meetings know what the children and young people have been doing at the event. This sort of positive communication is just as important as sharing difficulties and problems.

Maintaining links with children and young people who move away

Children and young people will sometimes move away from the meeting. They might go because they leave home for work or higher education, because they go away to boarding school, or because of a family break-up. In these and other situations the meeting may feel that it is appropriate to keep in touch.

A move away may follow a period of irregular attendance, making it difficult to build or maintain good channels of communication. The meeting can show that it still cares for the child or young person in a number of ways, for example:

- The impending move may be discussed in children and young people's meetings if appropriate.
- The young person should be asked if they would like the preparative meeting in the area to which they are moving to be informed of their address and something of their situation. If so, letters should be sent to the convenor of overseers or the clerk, with a copy to the young person.

- A small gift, such as a book token, *Quaker faith & practice* or a subscription to a Quaker publication may be given when the person leaves. A *Book of meetings* might also be helpful.
- A 'welcoming' card could be sent to their new address.
- It might be appropriate to continue to send birthday cards.
- Students might change addresses frequently, but e-mail can be an alternative way to contact them
- If the young person has a Linked Friend then that contact could be maintained.

Business meetings

> *Our shared experience of waiting for God's guidance in our meetings for worship and for church affairs, together with careful listening and gentleness of heart, forms the basis on which we can live out a life of love with and for each other and for those outside our community.*
>
> Qfp 10.03

Our way of conducting business is an integral part of our faith in practice. It is important that at least some adults who are involved with children and young people are also involved at all levels in the business processes of the Society.

Children and young people themselves should also be given the opportunity to learn about the Quaker business method and to try it for themselves.

- How are children and young people involved in business processes of your meeting?
- What decisions might be appropriate for a special business meeting involving children, young people

and representatives appointed by preparative meeting? Examples might include what colour the children's room should be painted, nominations of representatives to special events, or a choice of activities within the children's programme.

- How can children and young people develop their responsibility for organising, running, facilitating and clerking their 'own' events or groups? How can they learn to use Quaker processes? Young people have planned and clerked Junior Yearly Meeting, and played a full role on many Quaker Life committees: training and support are offered, but the belief in the ability comes first.

This way of working with children and young people, helping them to be responsible, is harder work than doing it all to them and for them yourself. It is a different way to work, difficult, challenging, but in the end more fruitful. To see people developing, to watch while they learn, to wait while that of God grows and blooms, is the satisfaction and blessing of this work.

Conclusions

> *Are there not different states, different degrees, different growths, different places?... Therefore watch every one to feel and know his own place and service in the body, and to be sensible of the gifts, places, and services of others, that the Lord may be honoured in all, and every one owned and honoured in the Lord, and no otherwise.*
> Isaac Penington, 1667 Qfp 10.27

Children and young people are not only the future of the Society of Friends, they are a vital part of its present life. The meeting should be a place where they can learn to celebrate their differences, abilities, and potential, and where they can grow in the spirit alongside their older fellow pilgrims. We are all challenged to help children and young people to develop the confidence and ability to make their own spiritual and emotional journeys. This booklet has only provided the first seeds in thinking about how we care for our children and young people, but we hope it can encourage us all to meet that challenge.

Appendix 1
Some questions

Examples of the types of questions which have arisen during discussions with elders and overseers.

1) What do we do if we have just one child at meeting?

Enjoy this time to get to know the child better and to appreciate him or her as an individual. Ideally, even when there is only one child in meeting, there will still be two adults. This is important and beneficial, not out of proportion. The children's meeting is an opportunity for spiritual discovery and sharing, and it will be useful for a child to have more than one perspective. Having the undivided attention of two adults for forty-five minutes can also be a very affirming experience. Remember, this is a meeting for worship, too, though it may take an unfamiliar form: the adults should not feel they are missing out.

From a child protection point of view it is important to have two adults even when there is only one child as this arrangement may help to avoid alleged or actual inappropriate behaviour. Whatever the number of children in the group, if it is necessary to rely on only one adult then sensible steps should be taken to ensure that there is back-up in case of accident or emergency. For example, it may be possible for children's meeting to take place in a space which is visible from the main meeting room, or for a connecting door to be left open. Creative thinking can ensure that adults and children are protected.

2) How do we cope with a small group of children of widely differing ages?

What is provided at children's meeting on a Sunday has to be put into the wider context of what the Society provides for children of all ages. At children's meeting older children can help younger ones but they will also need opportunities at other times to be with their peers. Activities at a monthly, general, or yearly meeting level will provide this opportunity.

There are a lot of practical, creative, imaginative and worshipful activities which can be undertaken by different age groups at their own level. Ideas which work well with a wide age range include cooking, responding to music, a story, creation and construction using paint, pens, clay, paper or other materials.

One meeting always has a lower table and a rug with construction and soft toys, picture books and drawing materials available for their youngest to be happy whilst older children are discussing and pursuing their own ideas. The young ones can then join in at their own level or not as they feel comfortable. Storytime can be set at the youngest level but is usually enjoyed by all. CYPC has a simple leaflet on *Working with a wide age range* and more ideas can be found in *Opening doors to Quaker religious education*. See pages 43 and 44 for more information.

3) What if children or young people only attend occasionally?

For various reasons children and young people may not attend meeting every week. Programmes have to be flexible and it may make sense to offer a series of 'stand alone' sessions which can be enjoyed on a one-off basis. Alternatively, one meeting has found it useful for every child to have a folder in which to keep unfinished work to continue next time. This also emphasises the importance of each person to the meeting and avoids the need to rush to finish something before joining the adults in worship. An ongoing theme that stretches over one or two months, with suitable source material for anyone to pick up something at any point, is useful.

Meeting each fortnight rather than each week has helped some meetings to concentrate the attendance of children and young people so that they can enjoy each other's company. Making contact with children/young people and/or parents individually to inform them of particular activities can give encouragement. Activities which build the whole meeting community can draw children and young people in. Someone can also maintain contact on behalf of the meeting – perhaps a Linked Friend, one of the people – young or older – present at the missed occasion.

Children & Young People's Section can offer more advice about all three of these questions. Ask about a visit from the Travelling Team to discuss your meeting's needs.

Appendix 2
Specific appointments
in local meetings

The following functions are important in the pastoral care of children and young people and they may be fulfilled by making specific appointments. Meetings may not make use of all these possibilities, or may decide to distribute some of the responsibilities in different ways. Sometimes, a few people have to carry out all the tasks, combining the roles. Circumstances in meetings vary, and overseers need to adapt guidelines rather than see them as a rigid formula. Understanding the principles, sensitivity and common sense along with an open discussion should lead to detailed guidelines that meet the needs of a particular meeting, and help them to keep the functions clear. In particular, the independent role of the children's overseer must be safeguarded. All the functions can be carried out safely, provided those responsible read and discuss *Meeting safety*.

This information may be particularly useful to nominations committees, as well as to those responsible for oversight and eldership.

Monthly meeting children and young people's resource co-ordinator

Monthly meetings are invited to appoint one or, preferably, two children and young people's resource co-ordinators.

In general, children and young people's resource co-ordinators have three tasks:

1. To encourage awareness of and support for the needs of children and young people in the monthly meeting.

2. To provide support and encouragement to those helping with the work with children and young people in the monthly meeting.

3. To be a point of contact beyond their own monthly meeting.

Resource Co-ordinators:

- are a point of contact for people throughout the monthly meeting who are involved in work with children and young people. It is hoped that resource co-ordinators would introduce themselves around the monthly meeting when they are first appointed;

- encourage a two way flow of ideas, experiences and best practice and a sharing of any problems within monthly meeting (MM), between other MMs, and between the MM and Children & Young People's Section (CYPS) in Friends House;

- receive and distribute information and new material from CYPS, for example a calendar of events for young people;

- work closely with the children and young people's committee within their monthly or preparative meetings;

- call people together to share and explore what they are doing with children and young people around the MM.

Children's overseer

Quaker faith & practice 12.13.e reminds us that 'each child and young person should be considered as an individual and not solely as a member of a family group'. The following tasks are similar to those of oversight of the whole meeting.

- If your meeting appoints overseers, each with a list, try to allocate family members to different overseers.

- In some meetings, overseers write a letter to each member and regular attender, 'Dear Friend, I have been asked to be your overseer, and I am writing to explain what this means...' How will you explain oversight, and make the connection, with the younger 'overseens'?

- If you have a corporate system of oversight, consider how families with children are placed in the link, loop or web. A geographical linking of neighbours may not be appropriate for the young.

- In a small meeting, you may not have much choice! If one person is responsible for the oversight, in whatever way, of one family, make sure he or she can be trusted not to share information that should be kept confidential.

- It might be helpful to discuss confidentiality in the whole meeting anyway, and to make use of the noticeboard or newsletter to set out the guidelines for all to see.

- Alternatively, one or two Friends, especially in a small meeting, could be appointed to oversee several children, apart from their parents. Don't assume, however, that parents, teachers or helpers in the children's meeting will automatically take responsibility for oversight: don't overburden them.

- Whatever your meeting's system, you will want to respect the wishes of those to be overseen, including each child or young person. How will you find out how they want to be overseen, and whose list, link or loop they want to be on? Could they help the nominations committee write the role descriptions?

The most important function of the children's overseer is to be available as an independent person for children and young people to talk to.

Giving children and young people access to one or more independent people in the meeting gives children more rights and lessens the possibility of undiscovered abuse. In the preparative meeting, such a person could be an overseer for children, who does not have regular involvement in work with children and young people in the meeting, but who is well known to them and readily accessible to them.

Meetings should consider how to let young people know about their children's overseer. At Junior Yearly Meeting, walls get filled with pictures, flipcharts, messages and lists. Among them is always a poster about a complaints procedure, so participants know who to go to if needed.

The children's overseer should have had some training in listening to and responding to children who wish to disclose child abuse or talk about any other issues. This overseer could have a wider role in the meeting as an advocate for children, particularly for any children who are facing any kind of stress or difficulty in their lives, although this role should by no means be restricted to a children's overseer. For more details, see *Meeting safety*. Children & Young People's Section have details of ecumenical training courses which would be very appropriate for meetings.

Linked Friend
See Linked Friends, page 13 above, for full details.

A Linked Friend is an adult member of the meeting who takes a special interest in a particular child, over a much longer period of time than is possible for an overseer appointed for the usual triennium who may have a long 'list' of people to oversee. This continuity enables a comfortable, supportive relationship, with good communication, and an effective link to the meeting, to be built up even when attendance at meeting for worship is sporadic or the young person leaves home.

- The meeting as a whole, including children, young people and their parents, needs to discuss and approve the details of their scheme. Refer to *Meeting safety* at this stage, and make sure all are clear about any groundrules and back-up system. How will the system generally, and particular linkings, be reviewed?

- The co-ordinators invite people to say how they would – or would not – like to be involved.

- The co-ordinator(s) of the scheme then ask participating children and young people to name two or more people they would like to be linked with.

- After discernment, the co-ordinator(s) approach nominees, to see if they feel able to take on the responsibility.

Convenor of children and young people's committee

'The responsibility for providing each local meeting with the necessary resources for eldership and oversight rests with the monthly meeting, while much of the ongoing work is carried out in its constituent meetings', according to *Quaker faith & practice* 12.06.

Within any monthly meeting, there may be link groups for teenagers, representatives to Junior Yearly Meeting to be supported, resource co-ordinators, children's overseers, Linked Friends, regular helpers with children's meeting, parents, occasional volunteers, over-19s who help at camp and various other concerned people.

A monthly meeting children & young people's committee, as suggested in *Qfp* 4.03, can make sure that all this involvement is effective and safe without burdening individuals with unnecessary complexity. The convenor or clerk will be a first point of contact, a key person in co-ordinating, planning, informing, keeping people in touch with each other. The convenor needs to have a wider viewpoint, and an awareness of the whole monthly meeting community, and the ability to include the children and young people sensitively and appropriately. The convenor will see that proper minutes and records are kept.

The convenor is not, however, to do all the work! Indeed, the skills of clerkship and co-ordination may be more useful than major involvement with the children and young people.

At local meeting level, individuals may carry out several roles at the same time. However, it keeps matters clear if a separation is made between various roles and functions. A children & young people's committee with a convenor can be of great help, the responsibilities being similar to the monthly meeting convenor of a children and young people's committee.

APPENDIX 3
RESOURCES

Publications

To buy from the Quaker Bookshop (for contact details see page 45):

Advices and Queries, chapter one of *Quaker faith & practice*, 1995, available as a separate book.

Armstrong, Helen, *Taking care*, National Children's Bureau, 1997.

> Response to children, adults and abuse, for churches and other faith communities – an ecumenical resource to complement the Quaker *Meeting safety* QHS 2001. The essential guide for meetings, including health, safety, law, child protection, supervising volunteers, responding to crisis, resources.

Know your rights! Children's rights in plain English, UNICEF, 1995.

> Well-informed children are more able to keep themselves safe.

One way of helping – a practical introduction to counselling young people informally, National Youth Agency

> This book will not train you as a counsellor, but will help you to respond sensitively rather that make a situation worse.

Book of meetings

> Contact details for every Quaker meeting and group in Britain: new edition available every January.

Cohen, Richard, *Students resolving conflict*, Good Year Books, 1995.

> The help you need to transform student disputes into opportunities for positive growth and learning, through peer mediation – useful for Quaker groups.

Faber, Adele and Mazlish, Elaine, *How to talk so that kids will listen and listen so that kids will talk*, Avon Books, 1999.

Firm Foundations – Parts 1 and 2, CYPC, 1996. (new edition to take account of *Meeting safety* to be published in 2001)

> Do-it-yourself exercises to help meetings consider the basis of their spiritual, practical and personal work with children and young people

Fostering vital Friends meetings Part II, Friends General Conference, 1999.

> Two dozen photocopiable sheets in this comprehensive tool kit for Quakers include 'Queries from Young Friends at FGC Gathering 1997', 'Listening and decision-making activity', 'Answering that of God in our children'. Available from the Quaker Bookshop, or visit the website:
> www.quaker.org/fgc/publications

Green, Maxine and Christian, Chandu, *Accompanying*, National Society/Church House Publishing, 1999.

> Accompanying young people on their quest through all sorts of situations, pastoral, social, religious, spiritual – illuminating accounts of conversations.

Heath, Harriet, *Answering that of God in our children*,

Pendle Hill Pamphlet 315, 1994.

'Seeing my child as a wonderer with the potential of growing into goodness expands my understanding of that child.'

Lampen, John, *The peace kit*, QHS, 1992.

Everyday peace-making for young people

Leimdorfer, Tom, *Once upon a conflict*, QPS, 1992.

A fairytale manual of conflict resolution for all ages

Meeting the challenge, Board of Social Responsibility, Church of England, 1999.

How churches should respond to sex offenders.

Meetings safety, QHS, 2001 (replaces *Safeguarding children from harm* and *Health, safety and the law*).

Miller, Karen, *The crisis manual*, Floris Books, 1999.

A guide for teachers and carers of young children: a reference book with information, resources and possible responses for a variety of situations from illness in a child's family through abuse to homelessness, with a chapter on caring for the carer!

Oakley, Terry, *Developing the all age community*, CYPC, 1997.

Patterns of eldership and oversight, Committee on Eldership & Oversight, 1997.

Information and exercises to help meetings review the way they organize pastoral care.

Promoting positive behaviour, Head-Start-East, London, 1997.

Activities for preventing bullying in primary school, lots to learn for use elsewhere.

Prutzman, Priscilla and others, *The friendly classroom for a small planet*, New Society Publishers, 1988.

> Ideas and activities for developing a healthy, active, positive group; applicable beyond a classroom.

Pudney, Warwick and Whitehouse, Elaine, *A volcano in my tummy*, New Society Publishers, 1996.

> Helping children to handle anger

Quaker faith & practice, the book of Christian discipline of the Yearly Meeting of the Religious Society of Friends (Quakers) in Britain, 1995.

Religious Education Committee, *Opening doors to Quaker religious education*, FGC, 1999 and *Opening doors to Quaker worship*, FGC, 1994.

> Two comprehensive books full of workable ideas and inspiration

Stone, Mary K., *Don't just do something, sit there*, RMEP, 1995.

> A book on children and spirituality, already a classic in religious education.

Wells, Rosemary, *Helping children cope with divorce,* Sheldon Press, 1997.

Wells, Rosemary, *Helping children cope with grief,* Sheldon Press, 1998.

> Two sound, practical books (with useful resources and contact lists), for situations when those who have to help can feel so inadequate.

What can we say about sexual abuse?, Q-HAPSA.

> A booklet by Quakers, for Quakers.

When the wind changes, Divorce and changing family patterns project of Children & Young People's Committee, QHS, 2001.

> Young people's experiences of divorce and changing family patterns, in their own words. Learn how it felt, what helped, what a meeting might do, should not do; above all, listen.

Young person's guide to the Quakers ,Quaker Life.

> For the leaflet rack in your meeting house; make sure young visitors are offered these.

Youthwork handbook, QHS, 1994, (new edition to be published in 2001).

> Basic guidance, needed by everyone working with young people in meetings.

Free leaflets and lists from Children & Young People's Section or the Committee on Eldership & Oversight

Handouts for meetings

> A list of all the handouts, lists, games sheets and other papers available from CYPS, including those noted below

Books and packs for children's and young people's meetings

Divorce and changing family patterns – a resource list for Friends

Eldership and oversight: resources to buy

Monthly meeting children and young people's resource coordinators: guidance notes

Oversight and eldership: free or to borrow resources list

Resources for children's meetings

Resources for teenagers, link groups and summer schools

Working with a wide age range

CONTACT ADDRESSES

The address for all the central offices and services of the Religious Society of Friends (Quakers) in Britain is:

Friends House

173 –177 Euston Road

London NW1 BJ

Telephone switchboard: +44 (0) 20 7663 1000

Facsimile: +44 (0) 20 7663 1001

Website: www.quaker.org.uk

Particular departments can also be contacted directly:

The Quaker Book Shop (for all Quaker publications)

Telephone: +44 (0) 20 7663 1030

E-mail: bookshop@quaker.org.uk

The CYPC Travelling Team can be booked to run training events for those who work with children and young people. For information on the Quaker youthwork foundation course, contact details for resource co-ordinators, free leaflets and lists, advice, programme of events:

Children & Young People's Committee, Children & Young People's Section

Telephone: +44 (0) 20 7663 1013

E-mail: janetf@quaker.org.uk

For information, advice, training and publications on a wide range of oversight or eldership matters:

The Committee on Eldership & Oversight

Telephone: +44 (0) 20 7663 1023

E-mail: ql@quaker.org.uk

For free annotated lists of resources, and to borrow in person or by post books, games, videos and a wide range of resources, including parachutes:

The Quaker Life Resources Room

Telephone: +44 (0) 20 7663 1023

E-mail: ql@quaker.org.uk

For courses on working with children and young people, also all-age and family events, ask for a programme:

Woodbrooke Quaker Study Centre

1046 Bristol Road

Birmingham

B29 6LJ

Telephone: +44 (0) 121 472 5171

Fax: +44 (0) 121 472 5173

Web: www.woodbrooke.org.uk

E-mail: enquiries@woodbrooke.org.uk